Zetta

The Girl Who Knew She Wanted To Be A Missionary Nurse,
The Lady Who Was Wise And Witty To 101

Vivian Johnson

ISBN: 978-0-8059-7544-4

Printed in the United States of America

Second Printing

Dedication

To my sister, Martha, who taped Mother's stories and who with her husband, Bob, provided an environment in which our mother, Zetta, could flourish in the last thirty years of her life.

To Lester, the dad I adored, who taught me how to tell the stories of the extraordinary life into which he led our family.

To my brothers, Jimmy and Les, who left early for heaven, leaving me to record their stories.

To my husband, Norm, who was always so kind to my mother, Zetta.

To my children, grandchildren, great grandchild, nieces and nephews, who are proof of the promise in Psalms: "God's faithfulness endures to all generations."

Endorsements

"I was the neighbor boy who was led to faith in Christ in Zetta's Bible Club in 1917. Now a man in my nineties, I still recognize the influence Zetta had in my life."

– Ray Schulenberg, A founder of Youth for Christ and retired pastor

"I am Zetta's daughter who at age two and a half, stood beside my parents as they buried my little brother. To this day, I am profoundly touched that even in this time of grieving, my parents had true joy and great tranquility because of the honor they afforded the Word of God."

– Martha Huber Pritchard, Daughter

"I am the science teacher who was inspired academically and spiritually by a 93-year old student named, 'Zetta.'"

– Russ Quackenbush, High School Science Teacher

"I am the mother of two of the young children that were cared for by Zetta while I taught summer school. My life was deeply impacted when this lady who was fifty years older than I, became my mentor and friend."

– Beverly Garcia, Educational Technology Specialist (Ed.S)

"We are the grandsons who went off to the U.S. Naval Academy firmly grounded in the Word of God, much in part, because of a grandmother named 'Zetta.'"

– Lt. Col. Robert W. Pritchard, USMC
– Major James A. Pritchard, USMC

Excerpts

"While most people think that running boards on old trucks were for stepping up into the trucks or for carrying passengers who could not fit inside, Martha, Vivian and Les knew them as kneeling benches for their parents. Their parents' kneeling on the running boards will forever remain in the minds of the Huber children as an indication of the complete trust their parents had in God. That is what they saw. The prayer they heard was, "Lord, you're our only hope.""

"Years later they spoke of the indescribable feeling of going by the Statue of Liberty and then later returning to deck, finding nothing but ocean in every direction. The ship they were on had transported 3000 servicemen home, so each cabin, and even the ballroom, had beds that were three-bunks high. The December storms were wild, causing dishes to slide back and forth at mealtime. The children were allowed to steer the ship on the Atlantic and watch the Morse Code being blinked-out by passing ships in the dark. As there were still mines in the water, especially in the Mediterranean Sea, passengers wore life jackets with redcapped flashlights attached at all times. They arose to alarms at night, at which time all were to stand by the lifeboats on deck..."

"Zetta was continually learning new things. At age ninety-three, she took a bus weekly to a science class, where she used a microscope and watched as a cow heart was dissected. She took such an interest in the study of DNA that her instructor gave her a private lesson on the subject. This gentleman whom Zetta admired very much, later described Zetta as his '*Reader's Digest's* Most Unforgettable Character'."

Contents

Summary

Zetta, who was born in 1897 in Chicago, Illinois, knew from an early age that she wanted to be a missionary nurse in the jungles of Central Africa. Her wish came true when she and her husband, Lester Huber, lived in mud houses while working with the Azande people.

Leopards, pythons, driver ants and tropical diseases were all around them. When the Hubers' young son died of malaria, many of the Azandes gave up their idol worship and put their faith in the God whom they saw in the lives of these parents.

Though Zetta lived in unusual circumstances in her early life, it was in the last thirty years of her life that she became even more grounded in faith and curious for knowledge. She took control of her paperwork and health care decisions, and with a twinkle in her eye, fascinated and mentored children, teenagers, adults and peers. When Zetta was asked, at age one hundred, to what she attributed her longevity, one never knew if she might say, "God's Word" or "Kentucky Fried Chicken!"

From rescuing her son from an elephant trap to having her picture in color on the front page of the "New York Times," the story of Zetta's one hundred and one years will keep you interested from start to finish.

Zetta—The Child

In 1897 in Chicago, Illinois, a little girl with black curls and big blue eyes was born. Her name, "LeZetta," was shortened to "Zetta" all her life. She was the oldest of nine children born in the following order: two girls and a boy; two girls and a boy; two girls and a boy. As each baby was born, Zetta had to stay home from school to help her mother care for her brothers and sisters.

To care for his large family, Zetta's father painted houses and in their own yard planted a big garden. Zetta helped her father wash and polish the vegetables, then took them around the neighborhood on a cart to sell them. It made her feel so good to come home and fill her mother's hands with the coins she had received. She also brought home firewood which carpenters had left for her.

One day when her mother sent her to the grocery store with a list of things to buy, she added a scribble to the bottom of the grocery list.

The man at the store asked, "What does this little scribble mean?"

"That means candy," replied Zetta.

Her father took her to Canada to visit her grandparents when she was a small child. She recalled looking up into the night sky and seeing Haley's Comet. Back in Chicago, she loved to pick wild flowers in the prairies near her home.

At age twelve, when she put her faith in Jesus Christ, she decided that she wanted to be a missionary nurse in the jungles of Africa, where she could work with people who had not heard of God's plan.

Zetta—The Young Lady

When Zetta was 19, she started a Bible club in her home, for her eight brothers and sisters and the neighborhood children. One girl later went as a missionary to India and another went to Africa. One boy became a pastor as well as one of the founders of Youth for Christ who scheduled the young Billy Graham for speaking engagements with that organization. When Zetta borrowed folding chairs and a pump organ for her club from the big Moody Church, a man there noticed what she was doing. Zetta later was told that she was the inspiration for the worldwide organization, Child Evangelism Fellowship, which this gentleman founded.

Zetta took three buses to get to work at Sears, where she worked in the candy department. One day at a birthday party she saw a young man named Lester Huber, walk in. She liked how he treated people. Lester, who knew immediately that he would some day marry her, asked to take her home. He gave her long-stemmed roses and Fannie May chocolates, then made payments on a diamond ring. They walked for miles or rode double-decker buses while talking about getting married and going to Africa. Lester worked in the law office of the Bell Telephone Company in Chicago.

They attended Moody Bible Institute (MBI), where Lester studied to be a pastor and Zetta studied to be a missionary nurse. They also took the Tropical Disease Course. After Zetta's graduation from nurses' training, she had only two weeks to prepare for their wedding. When it was time for the wedding to start at Moody Church, where 300 guests were waiting, Lester was not there. Zetta had no doubt he would arrive, because he was always on time, always there when he said he would be.

He was stuck on the other side of a drawbridge of the Chicago River. After their lovely but simple wedding, they attended a supper for sixty guests at Zetta's home, where earlier she had shown her young sister where the "decoy" suitcase was hidden. Just as Zetta had hoped, her sister told her brothers, who Zetta knew would try to steal her real suitcase. Knowing they would also try to stop the get-away car, Lester and Zetta left through the back door and escaped in their aunt's new Hudson.

A doctor and his wife heard that Lester and Zetta wanted to be missionaries. They gave them $1500 to buy the supplies they would need to take to Africa, money for their tickets, a folding organ and cans of food.

They sailed from New York on the Majestic through the November storms to France. On a train to Paris, Lester befriended a son of a countess. Later the couple asked him to recommend a hotel in Paris. They should have known that this rich man would direct them to an expensive hotel! They stayed there one night and could afford only oatmeal for breakfast.

In Paris and in Geneva, Switzerland, they learned French so well that they were later asked by Africa Inland Mission (AIM) to communicate with French-speaking officials on behalf of the mission. They toured the Palace of Versailles, Notre Dame and Luxemburg Gardens; and they especially enjoyed touring the cathedrals in each town they visited.

They sailed from France to Egypt; then spent two weeks on the Nile River before landing at Juba, Sudan. They arrived at Aba, in the Belgian Congo (now Republic of Congo) during the missionary annual conference. The mission was asking for volunteers to go to French Equatorial Africa (FEA), which is now called Central Africa Republic. After reading many encouraging verses in the Book of Deuteronomy, Lester and Zetta volunteered to go to this isolated area with its terribly rough circumstances, including disease, poor soil and mud houses.

In an old Chevy truck with wooden seats and no brakes, they headed for Zemio, in FEA, located on the Mbomo River, which divides FEA from the Belgian Congo (now Republic of

Congo). They had to take the long 950-mile way around to enter the colony because they did not have a permit to cross the river at Zemio. They traveled north on the one-lane dirt road during the day and slept at mission stations at night. Their ever-present sense of humor had them laughing as they sat on cots with umbrellas, their first night at Zemio, while the rain leaked through the grass roof.

Lester and Zetta Huber, next to the old Chevy

Zetta—The Missionary Nurse

Frequently missionaries are asked why they don't leave people alone who are "happy just as they are." Zetta and Lester found people who were gripped with fear, attempting to appease the evil spirits with offerings or to scare the evil spirits away from their villages by leaving rotten eggs or hot stones out for them. While on safari, Lester stopped at a village where the Azandes were worshipping a "good spirit." Somehow a large metal spike from a sailing vessel had been carried into the center of Africa. These people had molded it into a ring—hoping that the "good spirit" would go around in the circle, and thus remain in their village. Lester told them the story of the Spirit of God, from heaven who desires to enter each person's heart. The people were terrified of the thought of not continuing to worship the spirit in the ring. Months later several men appeared at the mission station holding the ring, stating that their whole village wanted to believe in the Son of God.

Believers memorized Scripture, sang hymns, prayed, tithed the money they received for working on the mission station and told the story of salvation to others. Many of them became examples to the missionaries in their discipleship. But like other Christian workers of their time and of today, the Hubers struggled for answers as to what of these people's culture should change, to fit in with what seemed to be Christian principles. Missionaries start a new station by locating near a government post so mail can be received weekly. Sometimes there was a store at the post, but in FEA the stores were limited to a few things like rock salt, cotton material and machetes. It was preferable to build on a hill to avoid the swamp and the potentially deadly insects and to be near a stream of water. Several hundred Azandes built their homes on the station. At Zemio there was a mud home for a missionary family and one for the single lady who worked mostly with the Azande girls and women. The houses had mud walls and floors, an elephant grass roof, wooden windows with screens, outdoor cooking, an outhouse, and kerosene lanterns for light. Baths were taken in tubs, or one could shower in a grass enclosure by pulling a chain on an elevated water can.

The original chapel, which was also used for a school, consisted of a large thatched roof with logs for seats. Zetta accompanied the singing on a pump organ, which was transported everywhere a group met. The Azandes learned to read and write in their own language and in French. They studied the New Testament, which had already been translated into their language, PaZande. They were great learners, quickly able to teach others at the mission or in villages miles away.

Zetta and those she trained to work in the dispensary worked out of a mud building. She recalled delivering forty-five African babies, most of whom arrived at night. Lester would hear someone at the door, coughing to get his attention. Zetta entered the mud hut, finding the mother by a fire on a grass mat with leaves. A newborn was washed and dressed in a shirt, and then received ointment for its eyes. Upon request from the parents, Zetta gave the babies Christian names. Otherwise the custom was to name the baby something related to circumstances, such as "Father of Hunger."

While there was an abundance of fruit--twenty-one kinds of bananas, pineapples, mangoes and oranges--very few vegetables made it through the poor soil. Canned sardines, baboon, fish and chicken provided meat, while peanuts, rice and potatoes were staples. Since cows were not available because of sleeping sickness, goats' milk or powdered milk was used. Most of the food and supplies had to be brought from the Belgian Congo.

Missionaries were so isolated in this area that letters from America meant everything to them. Zetta's mother wrote continually, always including Scripture. They felt that their family and friends through their love, prayers and financial support, had a significant part in the work they were doing.

The French government informed Lester that if missionaries wanted to remain in that area, they must build permanent buildings. Lester, whose experience was with the Bell Telephone Company and as a pastor, had no construction experience; so he and Zetta knelt in prayer and read the Scriptures in total dependence on their Lord, as was their pattern throughout life. They were quick to say that when they opened the Bible, they did not expect to point to a verse and do exactly what it said. However, when they did seek encouragement, guidance and strength from its pages, at this time, and later in "The Goats' Milk Story," they knew ahead of time that God would do something extraordinary for them.

They opened the Bible to Exodus and found the promise that God would give wisdom in building, with skilled stone masters, carpenters and craftsmen of every kind. This was all fulfilled as the eight-room brick home was built. With giant handsaws, carpenters sawed the wood from trees in the jungle . Masons cut stones and laid the foundation. Bags of cement were mixed with water. The dirt from anthills, rich with saliva, was perfect for making bricks. The Azandes stomped the mud for days while chanting; then the dirt was set in a wooden mold the size of a shoebox for burning in a kiln. Since 1937 the missionary homes, hospital, schoolhouse and chapel stand as a testimony to God's faithfulness to a man and a woman who were utterly dependent on God for every great and small thing in their lives.

Dangerous and unusual animals were a big part of their lives. One night an army of possibly 10,000 driver ants marched into their house, looking for sugar. Being young and foolish, Lester and Zetta thought they could stop them with a blowtorch at the front door! The ants were scattered all over the house, causing them to have to sleep elsewhere that night. While the Africans used spears to hunt for meat, it was sometimes necessary for Lester to use his gun to protect from snakes and leopards. One fifteen-foot python swallowed a goat. When it was time to divide up the python steaks, the people wanted Lester to do it, asking him to make each piece of equal size for them. At another time a python of the same size was killed and hung from a high pole for a picture. Zetta was standing next to it until rigor mortis set in and the snake began to curl. Zetta was absent from that picture!

A trap was set for a leopard that had been hurting the Africans in the area. It got a foot in the trap and leaped up into a tree, trap and all. The people wanted to throw rocks and spears at it while yelling, "You killed my aunt." Lester shot it once in the head and thus preserved the beautiful skin. Those were the days that skins, as well as ivory and ebony, could be taken out of the country.

Lester was an avid baseball and football fan. He never gave up on the Chicago Cubs and the Chicago Bears. One day, knowing that Southern Methodist University (SMU), where he had attended, was scheduled to play Notre Dame, he fiddled and fiddled with the radio he had been given. In the past he had not been able to get any stations in the USA, only Europe. He got the game! Fearing he might lose it, he cradled the radio in his arms without moving it the entire time. SMU won 7-0! His family never forgot the smile on his face.

Zetta—The Mother

Six weeks before Zetta delivered her first child, Martha, she rode to Aba, in the Belgian Congo, with a couple who were also expecting a child. Lester remained at Zemio, working and teaching until just before the birth. They were so proud of their beautiful baby with dark hair, born at high noon. Zetta was required to remain at Aba two months before returning with the baby. Lester purchased a motorcycle with a sidecar for the five-day trip back to Zemio, first, through grassland where elephants and the most dangerous of animals, the buffalo, could be seen from the road. Then they went through jungle area which was inhabited by leopards, baboons and pythons. The Africans wove a basket for Martha in the sidecar.

One day a rocker bolt came off the motorcycle, causing it to go off the road into a tree. This was in an area where, if one should meet a truck, everyone would get out and ask what on earth they were doing there, and where on earth they were going! While Zetta and Martha sat under a mosquito net, the couple prayed that God would send someone their way to help them lift the motorcycle back onto the road. In time, a mail runner appeared. Lester asked him if he would ask for help when he reached the next village. A group of women appeared. The men were all out in the jungles collecting rubber. The women helped push the cycle back on the road, where Lester was able to put it back together. They arrived at the border between Congo and FEA, where crickets screeched in the dark. Due to the dry season, the river was too low for the pontoon to come across for them. From the FEA side the Africans came over in a dugout canoe, first taking Zetta and Martha across the hippopotamus and crocodile- infested river. They were welcomed on the FEA side with torches. Lester and the motorcycle arrived in the next canoe. Arriving at the mud house at Zemio, they found boxes containing baby gifts from two baby showers that had been given in America on their behalf.

Their second child was Jimmy, who at fifteen months of age, died of pneumonia and malaria. While the grief was overwhelming, none of the family ever heard them say anything negative about their loss. People spoke only of God's comfort as the couple buried their baby in a trunk in the jungles and spoke of Lester's message at the funeral of joy and hope. He spoke in PaZande for the Africans and in French for the official from the government post. The several hundred people who had gathered for the service were from the mission station at Zemio and from miles away--having heard of it by drumbeat sent from village to village. Many responded at that time to the God whom they saw in the lives of these parents.

Jimmy Huber

When their third child was expected, a decision had to be made whether to make a trip to the doctor in the Belgian Congo or whether to deliver in the mud house at Zemio. When Zetta read the verse in the Book of Isaiah that says, "I will bless your offspring," she knew it would be all right to remain at Zemio and be assisted by the French doctor, who promised to remain in the area for the birth. Each birthday thereafter Vivian was reminded by her mother of that verse. Vivian would reply: "Yes, it has come true--I have truly been blessed."

Lester, Zetta, Martha and Vivian lived in their new brick home for five months before leaving for furlough. During this time they saved one can of powdered milk for the long trip out of Africa. That can was all the milk they had. Their goats were dried up, and a yellow fever scare had prevented the Field Director from entering FEA with the fifty- pound drum of powdered milk they had ordered. An Azande mother with septicemia could not nurse her baby, and Martha needed milk as well. Zetta went to her knees to pray. In Proverbs, Zetta read the words: "Thou shalt have goats' milk enough for thy food, for the food of thy household and for the maintenance for thy maidens." Zetta found Lester and told him, "We're going to have goats' milk."

A message came from a merchant at the government post, stating that he had gone up into the Chad and purchased a herd of goats from the Arabs. He was leaving on a trip and wondered if the missionaries could use the milk from his herd during his absence. Each day a young boy made the eight-mile round trip to pick up the milk. The merchant returned just as the Hubers were scheduled to leave for the coast of Africa.

Memories of the trip to Kampala, and then Mombasa, included sterilizing water for the can of powdered milk that they were able to save for the trip, hanging diapers up to dry and seeing Mt. Kilimanjaro. They described the trip across the Indian Ocean as "hot as a Turkish bath." In Singapore sailors aboard USA battleships cheered wildly as one missionary on the ship took an American flag and waved it towards them. In Malaysia they had tea in a merchant's mansion. Ebony, ivory and jade were everywhere. At a hotel in Japan, kimonos and toothbrushes awaited them. Lester was sent to the store for medication for five-month old Vivian, who with the others on board, had to be vaccinated because of a smallpox outbreak. In Japan, Martha saw for the first time a boy on skates and said, "There goes a boy on slipperies."

On the trip when playing with other children, she quickly changed from speaking PaZande to speaking English. Arriving in San Francisco, the family visited friends and supporters on the West Coast before heading to Chicago, where their family members met them at the train. They were shocked at how yellow Zetta's skin was from the tropical diseases and medications. She could hardly wait to get to her childhood home where her dear mother was waiting for her.

While on furlough, a son, Les, was born. When working in Dallas, Texas, Lester was able to attend Dallas Theological Seminary and Southern Methodist University. He also led the young married couples' Sunday School class at Scofield Memorial Church. This group of people became lifelong friends and supporters and their southern hospitality was enjoyed immensely. The Huber children sat for hours, it seemed, after dinner at various homes, listening over and over again to the wonderful stories of Africa.

Lester Huber

In 1945, after the war, it was decided that the family, including Martha, approximately twelve, Vivian, almost eight, and Les, six, would return to Africa. The Hubers took the train from Dallas to Chicago, where they stayed with relatives and attended Moody Church. Lester and Zetta took more French at Wheaton College. While at the AIM headquarters in New York, they got their inoculations and then crossed the scary gangplank to the

Santa Rosa, on which they sailed for three weeks. Years later they spoke of the indescribable feeling of going by the Statue of Liberty and then later returning to deck, finding nothing but ocean in every direction. The ship they were on had transported 3000 servicemen home; so each cabin, and even the ballroom, had beds that were three-bunks high. The December storms were wild, causing dishes to slide back and forth at mealtime. The children were allowed to steer the ship on the Atlantic and watch the Morse Code being blinked-out by passing ships in the dark. As there were still mines in the water, especially in the Mediterranean Sea, passengers wore life jackets with red-capped flashlights attached at all times. They arose to alarms at night, at which time all were to stand by the lifeboats on deck. During the day, it seemed, the children had the run of the ship, playing cops and robbers. Martha learned chess from the teenagers on board, while the younger children played Parcheesi.

Early one morning Lester took the children to the deck for a most unforgettable experience: seeing the Rock of Gibraltar looming up from the sea in the fog. They landed at Alexandria, Egypt, and took a train to Cairo, where the family stayed for two weeks at Assuit, a large orphanage. They rode camelback up to the Great Sphinx and by the light of magnesium strips, climbed up the highest pyramid, the tomb of King Cheops. The two-week trip up the Nile River provided indelible memories: having fresh fish for the first course of each meal, getting off at sunset to tour the monuments to Rameses the Great, watching the captain shoot crocodiles during hunting season, seeing hundreds of hippopotami clog the narrow river and watching elephant herds near the banks. During the trip, Vivian became seriously ill with bacillary dysentery. It was decided that if she did not improve, she and Zetta would have to get off at a hospital along the way. Vivian's parents knelt beside her bunk bed to pray. Within a day she was completely well. The family were able to continue on to Juba, Sudan, where they boarded a diesel truck and rode in the hot African sun to their mission school at Rethi, in the mountainous area of the Belgian Congo.

Every time the children left their parents, immense lumps in their throats inevitably turned into tears streaming down their faces. Les was only six years old when the children first stayed at boarding school for three months at a time, while their parents worked in FEA. While the children thought that the separation was hardest on them, Zetta later told them that when they left, she fell to her knees. Lester, whom the children had never seen cry, said he would put his head on the steering wheel and sob as he drove away after leaving them at Rethi. While crying themselves to sleep at night from homesickness and trying to "make it on their own" in those early years was extremely difficult, the children chose in later life to look back on these experiences as valuable preparation for their own ministry for Christ. It made them very sensitive to the lonely and to people who "did not belong."

Another thing which turned out to be a blessing was that they memorized large portions of Scripture (sometimes as punishment), and Vivian was always sorry to have to admit, that for that reason she knew just about the whole Bible! To this day the Hubers enjoy memorizing Scripture. As a result of their time in Africa, they became extremely appreciative. After all the years of outhouses and catalogs with lizards hanging out the pages, they were so grateful for indoor plumbing and soft tissue paper.

Approximately sixty missionary children lived in dormitories with houseparents. They had an excellent education in a two-room schoolhouse, especially in reading, writing and Bible. A highlight of the term was the mid-term picnic. The children piled into trucks and headed for the pine forest, knowing that the term was half over and they would soon be heading home!

Lester and Zetta were the furthest parents from Rethi when they started a new station at Rafai in FEA. This was a six-day trip by truck. Different fathers took turns picking up and delivering, up to fifteen children to and from Northern Congo and FEA. The children rode on top of their trunks in the back of open trucks. At the mission station each night they were given a fresh canteen of water and a lunch. The carrots got so soft from the equatorial sun that they could tie them in knots. The children wore helmets and as the helmets blew off, one by one, the children pounded on the cab for the driver to stop for them to be retrieved. There were no gas stations, so gas was carried in a metal barrel in the truck. To go to the toilet, girls went up the road and boys went down the road.

On one occasion, in the grassland area of Congo, when his parents were driving, Les did not return to the truck. When the parents heard a voice calling out, they found Les down a deep elephant trap, in a hole that had been dug by the Africans and then covered with elephant grass. A tire with a rope attached had to be lowered to get him out! On one trip, with just their family, many flat tires occurred. Lester was out changing tires while the rest of the family stayed in the cab, drinking sweetened condensed milk and thus drawing all the bees of the jungle to attack poor Lester!

How often the children recalled that their parents were told at the border of a colony that they could not cross over for some reason or another. Those parents always knelt to pray. While most people think that running boards on old trucks were for stepping up into the trucks or for carrying passengers who could not fit inside, Martha, Vivian and Les knew them as kneeling benches for their parents. The parents' kneeling on the running boards will forever remain in the minds of the Huber children as an indication of the complete trust which those parents had in God.

At home, the children spent their time riding bikes, reading and helping Lester and Zetta with the missionary work. When their belongings did not arrive from the United States for fifteen months, Vivian made a doll out of a hot water bottle by drawing a face on it and wrapping it in a towel. In the evenings they did puzzles and played games by lantern and later, by the one light bulb hanging in their living room, thanks to friends who had given them a generator. The arrival of the missionary barrel was a time of hope, which quickly changed to laughter.

While family and friends sent useful things that the family

could use, some organizations sent old clothes from which the zippers and buttons had been removed. The Hubers never did know what to do with one old high heeled shoe they received, without the mate. A friend in the States suggested later that they could have used it for traversing around the side of a hill! One time they received one hundred gravy-stained ties which were given to the Azande men. The men wore them on their bare necks--quite a sight with a loincloth! The ties should probably have been given to the women, since an Azande woman wore only a leaf!

At age fifteen, Martha left Africa by ship for her Junior and Senior years at Hampden DuBose Academy in Florida. Vivian joined her there as a freshman, having flown from Central Africa over the Sahara Desert to Paris. When touring Paris with a group from the plane, Vivian noticed that more people were looking at her than at the Eiffel Tower. Could it have been because in 1950 everyone else was wearing a dress to the ankles and she was dressed in a missionary-barrel suit that came only to her knees? At least her suit had been pressed with a charcoal iron before she left the jungles. Though she was "in" with her used saddle shoes; she had not gotten the message that the style at the time was to wear them dirty! She had gotten hold of some white shoe polish, causing her to lose out on her one opportunity to be in style! Her hair was still wavy from all the braiding in the braid line at Rethi. Heading for an ice-cream cone at a drugstore in New York (an event she had dreamed of for years), she saw people still staring at her. This time could it have been because of the pink cotton undershirt that showed through the white eyelet top she was wearing?

Besides separation from their parents for several years, the hardest part for missionary children returning to the States was engaging in "small talk" along with not having their own, acceptable clothes to wear. But Martha, Vivian and Les made a decision to recall their hardships with humor and purpose instead of with bitterness.

Zetta, Lester and Les returned to the United States in 1951, where friends who were Buick dealers met them at the dock in New Orleans with a classy Buick for them to use. Zetta worked as a nurse while Lester pastored churches or taught French and English in colleges. Martha, Vivian and Les attended MBI and college, then Martha and Vivian went on to nurses' training.

Zetta was at the side of her son, Les, when he died at age fifty from a brain tumor. Again, as with the death of her baby, Jimmy, and of her husband, Lester, she spoke only of hope and heaven.

Les, Vivian, Zetta, Martha, and Lester Huber

Zetta—The Centenarian

When Zetta's husband died, the family wondered what future and purpose there would be for her. What they saw was a lady who took up the spiritual banner for the family, prayed daily for them and kept in touch with African believers. Children whom she had cared for while she was working full-time in her eighties, flew across the nation to visit her. She was the belle of the ball at her grandsons' military balls. She was deeply appreciative of the consistent kindness shown by her children's spouses, her grandchildren and her great-grandchildren.

Zetta was continually learning new things. At age ninety-three, she took a bus weekly to a science class, where she used a microscope and watched as a cow heart was dissected. She took such an interest in the study of DNA that her instructor gave her a private lesson on the subject. This gentleman whom Zetta admired very much, later described Zetta as his *Reader's Digest's* Most Unforgettable Character."

She became very excited over any new invention. Her son-in-law, an aerospace engineer, had briefed her on the Super Collider, which was being developed in Texas. Months later Zetta greeted her daughter breathlessly at the door with: "Vivian, news of the greatest thing that's ever happened, besides the light bulb and the telephone--oh, except for Jesus dying on the cross--has just come on T.V.!"

She was up at five in the morning on the day of Presidential elections, to get ready to go to the polls to vote for Ronald Reagan and, later, for George Bush. On a visit to Washington, DC, she walked the entire mall, only getting short of breath when walking up the Capitol steps. When in line for the White House tour, she said, "I *must* go to the restroom."

Her daughter replied, "How can we? We'd have to walk all the way around to Lafayette Park and miss our tour."

A very kind guard led Zetta and her daughter up the driveway to the Reagan White House. As Zetta sat in the stall of the bathroom that gleamed with gold, she commented, "Isn't this nice of Nancy?" On her one hundredth birthday, she received a lovely letter and an autographed photo from Nancy Reagan, which she kept on her dresser with her family photos.

If asked to move faster, she'd say, "They never let me act my age." Late in life she lost sixty pounds on the "Fit for Life" program. When asked her date of birth, everyone in the doctor's office would look up when she answered: "October 16, 1897." On asking Zetta what she did for exercise, the nurse was alarmed when the patient answered: "The trampoline." The nurse envisioned Zetta doing cartwheels in mid-air!

Zetta's eyes danced as she threw wild flowers over a railroad trestle in Chicago, as she had done when six years old. She sounded like a girl of sixteen when she described how a gentleman at a retirement community party had told her she looked like a fairy princess in her pink chiffon dress. When the activity calendar said "ice cream cones," she and her friends planned for weeks in advance to attend, wearing their straw hats. All this brought to mind the Satchel Paige quote: "How old would you be if you didn't know how old you were?" When asked to what she attributed her longevity, one never knew if Zetta might answer, "God's faithfulness" or "Kentucky Fried Chicken"!

Zetta was thrilled to live with Martha and her husband in their home for four years after she lost her eyesight. Forty-eight people from nine states celebrated her one hundredth birthday in Phoenix. When a T.V. crew interviewed her as a centenarian, she began with, "Forbes Magazine doesn't know it, but I'm the richest lady in town"! The riches were in her faith, family and friends. As a missionary needing to leave household possessions to others each time she returned to America, Zetta would say, "I just wish I had something to leave my children," to which they would reply: "Mom, you're leaving us heritage."

A second crew asked to interview her. Thinking that each question she was asked might be her only opportunity to express her belief that what the world needs is to be grounded in the Scriptures, she always gave that same answer. When they asked, "Mrs. Huber, do you have one last thing you would like to say?" she replied: "Yes, but if I say it again, I might end up on the cutting room floor."

She had all her own teeth at age one hundred and one and flossed them after every meal! A visit to the dentist or the doctor was a social event for her. When she had cataract surgery on both eyes, she had such fun it appeared she would like to have had a third eye to be done! As she had done all her life, Zetta rose to her feet when a physician entered the room! She had great fun bantering in French with her primary physician. When an ophthalmologist informed her that she was legally blind, she took his hand and quoted from Isaiah: "I will bring the blind by a way that they know not. I will lead them in paths they have not known. I will make darkness light before them and the crooked things straight. These things will I do and not forsake them." The young physician had tears in his eyes as she quoted this.

She made sure that her wishes were expressed in her health care documents. She also arranged to donate her body to a university for research, to save on expenses and to help medical science.

Zetta lived at Crista Senior Community in Seattle for the last several months of her life. She loved to sit by the waterfall and patio garden that had been placed there in honor of the life of her son, Les. Staff members would come to her at all hours to ask her to pray for them. She answered, "I'm going to Faith/Rest that." She was referring to the practice described in the booklet, "Christian at Ease", by Robert Thieme, in which Christians believe what God says and rest in His promises to fulfill His Word. The staff were frequently returning with good news for her.

Having lost her hearing in her thirties from taking medication for malaria, Zetta heard nothing without a hearing aid. In fact, when caring for young children in her eighties, the only way she could awaken herself without wearing a hearing aid to bed was to attach a vibrating clock to her bed. With her blindness and deafness, she could not tell what time it was if she awoke during the night. Her daughters worked out a system with her by tapping the time on her wrist. At three in the morning, three little taps on her wrist would cause her to say, "Oh, it's three o'clock." It was also arranged that anytime in the future her daughters wanted to let her know they were there, they would tap on her wrist three times.

Zetta's family stayed with her the weekend she was going into kidney failure. They made sure that the staff gave her the frequent small doses of medication that allowed her to have deep, relaxed breathing--fulfilling Zetta's often-stated wish that she would always have enough air to breathe. Arrangements were made for Zetta and Lester's names to be placed on bricks on the sidewalk at MBI where they had become engaged so long ago. Their daughters also arranged for the tombstone marking their graves to read: "Together With Christ."

Zetta's last words were: "Jesus Christ died for our sins and is waiting for us at the right hand of God, in heaven; and He loves *you*."

"Yes, Mom," her family whispered, making three little taps on her wrist, and you were the first to tell us that."

Then this wise and witty lady who had lived in so many homes, but owned no real estate, who had worked so hard, but had had no stocks, left for her permanent home and all the rewards and treasures of heaven.

Zetta Huber on her 100th birthday

Made in the USA
Columbia, SC
14 July 2024

38388024R00024